ISBN 978-1-332-87667-9
PIBN 10297396

English
Français
Deutsche
Italiano
Español
Português

www.forgottenbooks.com

Mythology Photography **Fiction**
Fishing Christianity **Art** Cooking
Essays Buddhism Freemasonry
Medicine **Biology** Music **Ancient**
Egypt Evolution Carpentry Physics
Dance Geology **Mathematics** Fitness
Shakespeare **Folklore** Yoga Marketing
Confidence Immortality Biographies
Poetry **Psychology** Witchcraft
Electronics Chemistry History **Law**
Accounting **Philosophy** Anthropology
Alchemy Drama Quantum Mechanics
Atheism Sexual Health **Ancient History**
Entrepreneurship Languages Sport
Paleontology Needlework Islam
Metaphysics Investment Archaeology
Parenting Statistics Criminology
Motivational

STORK'S + DESCRIPTIVE + MANUAL

OF

Select Summer Tours.

FOR 1879, FROM

MARYLAND to MAINE

PASSING THROUGH TEN STATES

Visiting some TWENTY of the Coolest and most Picturesque Seaside and Mountain Resorts of America,

AT LOWER RATES THAN EVER BEFORE OFFERED FROM BALTIMORE TO

NEWPORT, R. I.
The Brighton of America.

NANTUCKET.
The Sea-girt Isle of the Atlantic.

MARTHA'S VINEYARD,
The city of 1000 cottages by the sea.

WHITE MOUNTAINS,
The Switzerland of America.

MOUNT DESERT,
The Island of Mountains—Etc., Etc,

700 MILES BY SEA AND SOUND.   1000 MILES BY RAIL.

WHERE SHALL I SPEND MY SUMMER HOLIDAY?

THE 1000 MILE EXCURSION of 1878, avoided the evils which had before been inseparable from Excursions. Starting upon either of *several* days, by *regular* trains and steamers, the extent of the trips, the pleasing variety of travel, the delightful places visited, and the unprecedented cheapness of the tickets, all combined to render it by far the most popular and successful enterprise of the kind ever undertaken in Baltimore. Among its patrons were included many of our leading citizens, with their families, and all were so well pleased that there has been a general request for its repetition the present season. In response to this, Two series of Select Tours have been organized, in which all the features which rendered the "1000 Mile Excursion" so exceedingly popular have been retained, and a number of new attractions added. No one will be able to find more charming and healthful resorts nor to reach them by more desirable routes than those furnished by these tours. At these favorite and famous summer haunts all the healthful sports of Driving, Sailing, Fishing, Bathing or Mountain Climbing, can be fully enjoyed. They who must practice economy, have in these tours unequaled facilities for obtaining the greatest amount of pleasure and benefit at the least expense. The price of tickets is lower than ever before offered, and arrangements have been made with leading hotels on the routes to accommodate holders of them at a liberal discount on regular rates.

This book is designed to be an Encyclopœdia of everything that it is desirable to know in reference to these tours.. Care has been taken not to exaggerate, but to keep within the truth and make it reliable in all respects.

REST AND RECREATION.

A wise economy of time or money will not omit a short summer vacation. In this climate it is as much a necessity as a luxury. One who works with mind or body or both, at business or study, requires relaxation, although he may not be sensible of it. The well need it to fortify them against disease and keep up their supply of strength and vigor. The delicate and invalid will often be more benefited by a trip involving change of scene, change of climate, air, diet, &c., than by swallowing any amount of medicine. The mind is strengthened and invigorated, and the spirits quickened by new and interesting experiences and adventure. It is of little use to go a few miles into the country. One should travel *a good distance from home* to realize these advantages. For the overtaxed body or brain, the cool and quiet rest of the sea girt island of Nantucket is invaluable. Weak nerves speedily grow strong here and at Martha's Vineyard, with its safe and delightful Sea bathing. The pure and exhilerating atmosphere of the White Mountains and Mt. Desert, offer unrivaled attractions to such as require or prefer the mountains.

Endorsements of the Excursion of 1878.

A very large number of intelligent people availed themselves of the advantages of the "1000 Mile Tours of 1878." Of these, nearly 400 were citizens of Baltimore, including a large proportion of our most prominent professional and business men, together with their families. There were also representatives from Pennsylvania, Virginia, and several of the counties of Maryland. All were delighted with the lines of travel and the places visited.— A complimentary expression of the general appreciation of the trip and its enjoyable features was tendered to the managers. Herewith are appended extracts from several letters received in reference to it:

YORK, PA., September 1st, 1878.

Manager of the 1000 *Mile Excursion :*

We desire to express to you our gratification at the many interesting and enjoyable features of the "*One Thousand Mile Excursion,*" and take pleasure in testifying to its *general excellence* of character and *management.* Signed by

HENRI WOLF WIEST.	E. C. BECK.	HON. THOS. E. COCHRAN.
HON. GEO W. HEIGES & WIFE.	CHAS. BRANT.	ELI J. MILLER.
RICH'D. E COCHRAN.	DAN. W. SCHALL.	W. S KENNY.
HON. JOHN GIBSON & WIFE.	D. W. CRIDER.	H. EBERT.
P. GRAY.	F. G. STARK, Hanover, Pa.	

From TILMAN SHUMATE, ESQ., Cashier Bank of Winchester, Va.

WINCHESTER, VA., August 16th, 1878.

Gentlemen—I beg to say that my trip to Nantucket was pleasant in every respect. To any one in search of health or recreation, I know of no trip offering the inducements of the one to Nantucket, over the delightful Fall River line, together with a week's sojourn in the quaint and interesting old town. Very truly yours, TILMAN SHUMATE.

From DR. J. J. WEAVER.

UNIONTOWN, MD., April 14th, 1879.

Dear Sir—You conferred quite a favor upon the community last season by getting up those excursions to Nantucket and Martha's Vineyard. More health and pleasure in so short a time could not be procured in any other way for the same amount of money. The sanitary condition of Martha's Vineyard and Nantucket furnishes to the most fastidious all that could be desired for the promotion of health and happiness. The lungs are exhilerated by the refreshing sea breeze from either direction. The exciting sport of blue and shark fishing, the novelty of the clam bakes, and the grateful and happy exercise of sea bathing, all tend rapidly to recuperate emaciated bodies, enervated nerves and exhausted mental faculties, which each one will soon realize by his firm and nimble step in his rambles by day and his sound refreshing sleep by night. Yours respectfully, J. J. WEAVER.

FREDERICKSBURG, VA., March 31st, 1879.

Dear Sir—Having made the excursion advertised by you last season, we recommend all parties who desire a pleasant and economical trip, to embrace the opportunity offered.— We were so much pleased with the trip that we purpose to repeat it this summer, and several others will join the party. Yours respectfully, JNO. F. GOLDMAN.
W. T. LOWERY.
JAS. T. LOWERY.

From REV. J. F. JENNISON, Pastor Lafayette Sq. Presb. Church.

BALTIMORE, March 29th, 1879.

W. L. STORK—*My Dear Sir*—It would be hard for any one who has never visited the old-time New England villages to realize the delightful contrast of quiet and repose presented by the quaint old town, Nantucket. To the weary brain of the hard-working minister, lawyer or business man, there is something extremely agreeable and refreshing in the deliciously cool ocean air, the perfect rest and the grand all-night sleep secured. Then the sailing and fishing on the smooth inlet or on the ocean itself; the splended catch of blue fish, or the haul of an enormous shark; the exhilerating hot or cold sea-bath; the clam bakes up at Wauwinnet; the pleasant ramble along the shores or over the breezy island; indeed it is hard to bring it all up to mind without longing that the time were come to be there once more again, to renew the delightful experiences and the agreeable companionships of last summer. Trusting that you may be even more successful than last season, I am, yours very truly, JOS. F. JENNISON.

W. L STORK, ESQ.,

Wilmington, Del., May 16, 1879.

Dear Sir.—Your Excursion of last summer, to Nantucket, Martha's Vineyard, Etc., I consider one of the most enjoyable of any on which I have gone.

The route itself is so well known, that it seems needless to say anything further in its praise; as to the excursion, the arrangements were very complete. The very low rates at which tickets were sold, should make another excursion still more popular than the last.

It gives me much pleasure to assure you of my satisfaction with the excursion of last year Yours Respectfully, A. G. ROBINSON, *Cashier Farmers' Bank.*

SYNOPSIS OF ROUTE

FROM

WASHINGTON, D. C., TO BALTIMORE, NEW YORK, NEWPORT, MARTHA'S VINEYARD,

NANTUCKET, BOSTON, WHITE MOUNTAINS, MT. DESERT, ETC.

In order to make through and close connections, the tourist will leave B. & P. Depot, Washington, D. C., at 8 35 A. M on either day, from July 14th to 17th, inclusive, for the First Series of Tours, and on either day from Aug 4th to 7th, inclusive, for the Second Series This train connects with the 9.55 A. M, train from Baltimore, without transfer of passengers The train passes over the Gunpowder and Bush rivers, crosses the Susquehanna at Havre de-Grace, on the great iron bridge, arriving at Wilmington, Del., 12.27 A. M., where refreshments can be obtained ; leaving at 12.41 winds around the city of Philadelphia, affording an excellent bird's eye view of it; passes alongside of the Zoological Garden's which are plainly seen on the right; through Fairmount Park, where the Centennial Exhibition was held, and now the seat of the permanent Exhibition. Then the train speeds on over the fine Railroad bridge across the Schuylkill to the Delaware river, which is crossed at Trenton, the capital of New Jersey. From thence it proceeds, crossing the Raritan river at New Brunswick, past Railway and Elizabeth to the manufacturing city of Newark, and finally to Jersey City by 4 38 P. M. Here the Brooklyn Annex Ferry Boat will convey passengers across the North river to the Fall River Steamers direct, arriving at pier 28 in New York at 4 55 P. M. Going aboard the steamer (either the *Providence* or *Bristol*) secure at once your berths or staterooms. Having disposed of your satchels, valises, and hand-baggage, you can have a wash in the elegant toilet rooms. We advise all tourists to stop and see New York, the great metropolis, on their *return* trip.

D. SWEENY'S HOTEL.

NEWLY FITTED UP,

ON THE EUROPEAN PLAN.

No. 21 Duane Street, Near Chatham,

NEW YORK.

ROOMS $1.00 PER DAY.   **Stationary Wash Stands in all Rooms.**

The Cuisine of this Hotel, cannot fail to please the most fastidious.

The Fall River Palace Steamer leaves at 5 P, M., *promptly*, passes around the Battery, giving a full view of the magnificent harbor of New York, the Forts, the new Colossal Suspension Bridge now being constructed across East River to Brooklyn, the Prisons and Insane Asylum on Governor's and Blackwell's Islands, through Hell Gate, past Flushing, Fort Schuyler on the left, Willett's Point on the right, City Island 2d, Hart Island, Stepping-Stone Light-House, Execution Rock Light-House, Sands Point Light-House, then through Long Island Sound out into the Atlantic Ocean past Point Judith to Newport, R. I.,* reaching here about 2 A .M , and arriving at Fall River at 5 A.M. The tourist has time to take a light breakfast. Should your ticket read direct to Martha's Vineyard and Nantucket, step on board the Fast Express for New Bedford, (do not make a mistake and get on the Boston Express)—leaving at about 6 A. M. (Should your ticket read direct to Boston, instead of via the Vineyard and Nantucket, you will take the fast Express which leaves about 5 10 A. M., arriving at the Old Colony Depot in Boston, at 7 A. M.,) arriving at New Bedford 7 A. M. At New Bedford you take the Steamer for a ride of about 4 hours on the Atlantic Ocean, touching at Oak Bluffs, Martha's Vineyard, and landing in Nantucket about 11 A. M., (tourists after leaving New York, en route North, have the privilege of stopping at any of the places on their route, either going or returning.) Returning via Boston, leave Nantucket at 7.15 A. M., taking cars at Wood's Holl, and arrive at the Old Colony Depot in Boston about 2 P. M. Blue Horse Cars marked "Depots, Eastern R. R. &c.," run directly from in front of the Old Colony Depot to the Eastern R. R. Depot, and vice versa—about 20 minutes time from Depot to Depot.—Fare 6 cents. Tourists not going to Boston, return from Nantucket by same route, via New Bedford.

Those whose tickets include Boston now have the opportunity of seeing the sights of this great city. On your return South, leave the old Colony Depot at 6 P. M.. and arrive in New York city, via Fall River Steamers, at about 6.30 A. M. the following morning.

*Tourists for convenience should stop at Newport on return trip—go via Rail from Fall River,

For those whose tickets read to White Mountains direct, and to Mount Desert, via White Mountains and Portland, trains leave the Depot of the Eastern R. R. at 8 A. M., and 12.30 P. M., going through witl out change, via N. Conway to Fabyans, Wlite Mount. ains, arriving there about 3 P. M. and 7.00 P. M. From tl is point delightful excursions can be made to tl e top of Mt. Washington, Profile House and Echo Lake, Flume, Bethlehem, Littleton, Etc.

Tourists returning direct to Boston, leave Fabyans about 10 30 A. M. and 2 25 P. M. arriving in Boston about 5.30 and 9.30 P. M. Those going to Mt Desert via Wlite Mount. ians, leave Fabyans about 2 25 P. M. for Portland, arriving there about 6 30. The Mt. Desert Steamer of P. B & M. Steamboat Co., leaves Portland at 11 P. M. and reaches Mt. Desert about 10 A. M. the following day.

REMEMBER, Steamers from Portland to Mount Desert leave only on MONDAYS, TUESDAYS, WEDNESDAYS and FRIDAYS.

Those having tickets, reading to Mt. Desert direct, via Portland (omitting White Mountains) will take evening Train from Boston, leaving about 7 o'clock from depot of Eastern R. R., (Mondays, Tuesdays, Wednesdays and Fridays for through connection to Mt. Desert) arrive in Portland at about 11 P. M., making close connection with tl e Steamers City of Richmond or Lewiston, whicl leave Portland at 11 P. M. for Mt. Desert. The Cars run direct to the steamboat wharf. After a good night's rest on the steamer, arrive at Bar Harbor, Mt Desert, about 10 A. M. RETURNING, Steamer City of Richmond leaves Mt. Desert at 7.30 A. M., on Wednesdays and Fridays, arrives in Portland same day at about 5 P. M., connecting witl trains for Boston, arriving at 9.30 P. M. STEAMER LEWISTON leaves Mount Desert, Mondays and Thursdays, at 10 A. M., arriving in Portland same evening connecting with Pullman night train or early morning trains for Boston.

Tourists need not confine tlemselves to the close connections and rapid travel as here given, but can stop off when and where they please, according to the date and route indicated on their tickets.

What Will it Cost? Almost as Cheap as to Stay at Home.

Inquiry is often made as to what will be the entire cost of a trip Now this depends almost entirely upon the tourist. The extras are what swell the aggregate expense, and these can be regulated according to purse and pleasure. And then wlere parties of three or more go together the expense to each individual is much less than wlen one travels alone. The following estimate is not imaginary, but is based upon actual experience. It is calculated for the minimum cost of an economical tour of 12 days for one person:

Price of ticket—Tour A, Baltimore to Martha's Vineyard, Nantucket and return....	13.25
(Lunch taken from home) Supper on Fall River Steamer..........................	.65
Breakfast...................... " " "	.85
One Week's board at Nantucket.,..	7 00
Excursion to Clambake at Wauwinet, with 18 mile sail, Fish Dinner, Surf Bath, &c.....	.90
A day at the fairy Island of Martha's Vineyard with its various attractions..........	2.00
A day at Newport, with 9 mile ride in coach along the Beach. &c....	2.50
Breakfast Dinner and Supper in New York.......................................	1.15
A Ride in Mid Air on the Elevated Railway to Central Park and return.............	.20
	28.00

Of course the expense can be increased ad libitum. Other tours of this series can be made at proportionately reasonable rates.

SIDE TRIPS.

MANHATTAN & BRIGHTON BEACHES, L. I., within easy access of New York City by Rail or Boat.—Round trip tickets about 50 cents.

BEVERLY to ROCKPORT, taking in any of the Cape Ann points, 70 cents each way. Carriages from NORTHAMPTON to RYE BEACH, 50 cents each way.

PORTSMOUTH to ISLES OF SHOALS, 75 cents eacl way.

WOLFBORO to CENTRE HARBOR and return, by Steamers on Lake Winnepesaukee, 75 cents each way.

FABYANS to PROFILE HOUSE and return (rail all the way) $4.00.

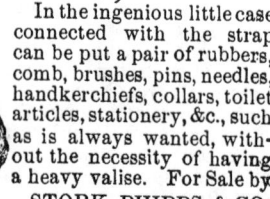

Items of Interest to Tourists.

FROM Maryland to Maine, a trip of 1700 miles—passing through Ten States.

VISITING the most famous islands of New England—Mt. Desert, Nantucket and Martha's Vineyard, and passing within forty minutes ride of the famous Isles of Shoals

THIS book tells you where to go, how to go, and what to see when you do go.

TAKE it with you and consult it carefully, for all information concerning these tours.

DO not stop (en route north) south of New Bedford.

IT is much better to visit other points on the return trip (en route south).

READ your ticket carefully, that you may thoroughly understand it.

WE can recommend the Hotels and Boarding-houses advertised in this book, knowing from personal experience, that they are as represented, having selected them with great care.

LADIES traveling alone can take this trip in perfect safety.

YOUR ticket for the first series of Tours entitles you to leave on any regular train from President-street Depot, Baltimore, (except the limited express) on tle 14th, 15th, 16th and 17th of July. For the second series, on tle 4th, 5th, 6th and 7th of August. Tickets good to return within 30 days.

NO Special Excursion Trains used on these tours.

IF you need advice or get in trouble in Portland Maine, call on Capt. Wm. Mitchell, at the depot of the Eastern Railroad, and agent of the Road. He is a most genial, unselfish and accommodating gentleman, and he will take pleasure in rendering every assistance to our tourists.

REMEMBER (in consulting your watches) the difference in time, as you proceed north. See page 6.

THESE Tours are specially advantageous for families, and select parties of ladies and gentlemen.

HALF Fare for children from five to twelve years of age.

YOUR ticket includes a berth on the Fall River and Mt. Desert Steamers.

GENTS should provide themselves with a *blue flannel* shirt and a suit of old clothes for sailing and fishing.

BOTH an umbrella and an opera or field glass will be useful to take with you.

TAKE as little baggage as possible.

TOURISTS' Tags for trunks and valises. Tourists' gummed labels for trunks. Tourists' handy correspondence papaterie, furnished with writing material,—strongly bound in canvass—just the thing for traveling—price 75 cents. The Plant Book, or Herbarium, for gathering ferns, leaves and flowers, with index and full directions, (see advertising page) all to be had of Stork, Phipps & Co., Fine Stationers and Printers, 220 W. Baltimore street, Baltimore.

HACK and Carriage fare in Boston is very cheap—fifty cents eacl passenger for a course within tle city proper, reasonable amount of baggage allowed. A tariff of the legal fare is in each carriage.

THE railroad ride to Edgartown, on Martha's Vineyard, seven miles along the sea beach, is very interesting. Round trip 50 cents.

WE are indebted to Messrs. Harper Bros., New York, for the handsome illustration of the Cliff Walk at Newport, R. I.

SUGGESTIONS.

A light lunch taken from home will be found acceptable on the train to New York.
State Rooms on Mt. Desert Steamer can be secured in advance by addressing Geo. L. Day, Portland, Maine, or J. W. Richardson, 214 Waslington Street, Boston.

To those desiring to engage State-rooms on Fall River Steamer en-route South, apply (as early as practicable) to No. 3 Old State House, Boston.

We would suggest tourists going in parties of from 4 to 10 persons; it reduces materially the cost of the trip to eacl person.

ALL TOURISTS en-route South from Boston, and desiring to go through to New York without stops, must take tle 6 P. M. Steamboat Train from Old Colony Depot to Fall River and thence by *Palace Steamer to New York City.*

WHAT TO WEAR.

Ladies who seldom travel are sometimes at a loss what to wear or take for a long trip. The *less* baggage tle better, usually, so it is best to wear sometling you are not afraid of spoiling, and yet looks well enough not to need changing. There is nothing better for a traveling suit tlan gray serge, which might be trimmed with tle same, a contrasting color, silk, or in any other of the numerous ways fashion allows this season. Of course gray serge is not by any means the only suitable material, and here as well as in the making and trimming, the figure, taste, and means of the wearer are to be consulted. A dress made of a material more easily soiled might be worn with safety if protected from dust by a linen ulster, and from rain by a waterproof. For pretty styles for traveling costumes write to the Butterick Pattern Agency of Baltimore, for a catalogue, and after selecting tle style, you can send for a pattern It is much better taste to be dressed over-plainly than over-fancifully, in traveling For a hat, anytling that is plain, from which dust can be brushed and which a shower would not spoil.

GENTLEMEN'S WEAR.

Linen dusters will be found convenient, and a light cloth cap to wear in the cars, that can be rolled up and put in the pocket at other times, will pay for the investment. Resist the temptation to take along an extra suit, as you will regret being burdened with baggage you cannot easily landle. Your portmanteau should contain a Bible, collars, cuffs, landkerchiefs, towel, brush and comb.

TABLE OF DISTANCES.

Baltimore to Philadelplia,........... 98 m.		Boston to Fabyans, White Mountains, 169 m.	
Pliladelplia to New York City,..... 88 m.		Wlite Mts. (Fabyans) to N. Conway,. 31 m.	
New York City to Boston,.. ....231 m.		N. Conway to Portland,............. 60 m.	
New York City to Newport,.........163 m.		Portland to Mt. Desert,...............110 m.	
Newport to New Bedford, ... 41 m.		Portland to Boston,...................108 m.	
New Bedford to Martha's Vineyard,.. 25 m.		Fall River to New Bedford,.......... 26 m.	
Martha's Vineyard to Nantucket,..... 37 m.		Nantucket to Boston,................109 m.	
New Bedord to Boston............. 94 m.			

Useful and Entertaining Books. Appropriate for these Tours.

NOOKS AND CORNERS OF THE NEW ENGLAND COAST,—*By Sam'l A. Drake.*—A volume of 460 pages, containing some 300 fine illustrations, over 100 of the latter, illustrating the very points on the route of these Tours—tlis book is specially interesting to tlose participating in the same. It gives a graphic description of NEWPORT, witl 51 illustrations; Nantucket with 17; Mount Desert with 27; Isles of Shoals with 19; Salem and Marblehead with 39. An appetizing book for travel, and refreshing to read in Summer. A useful book of reference. The fact of its being published by Harper Bros., New York, is a sufficient guarantee that it is as near perfect as a book can be. Price $3.50.

NEW ENGLAND—a Hand-book for travelers, a guide to tle chief cities and popular resorts of New England, and to its scenery and historic attractions. Price $2.00.

LORING, SHORT & HARMON'S GUIDE-BOOK for Mount Desert Island, Me. "Infinite riches in a little room," 75 cents

THE AMERICAN PLANT BOOK, for the preservation of Pressed Flowers, Ferns Sea-Weed, Grasses, Ivy, Mosses, &c. It is an excellent device for preserving flowers and grasses. See advertising page.

All of the above for Sale by STORK, PHIPPS & CO., 220 W. Baltimore Street Baltimore.

Difference in Time from Richmond, Va. to Portland, Me.

In consulting your Watches, allow as follows:
When it is 12 noon at Washington, D. C., it is 11.58 A. M., at Richmond, Va.—12.02 P. M., at Baltimore, Md.—12.07 at Philadelphia, Pa.—12.12 at New York.—12.24 at Boston.—12.27 at Portland Maine.

List of Stork's Summer Tours.

First Series.—Leave Baltimore, July 14, 15, 16 and 17.

Second Series.—Leave Baltimore, August 4, 5, 6 and 7, privilege of returning any time within 30 days from July 14th and August 4th, respectively. The usual amount of baggage allowed each passenger,—Checked through to Nantucket and White Mountains.

Privilege of leaving on any train (except the limited Express) from President Street Depot, on the above dates.

Baltimore to Nantucket.
(VIA NEW YORK AND NEWPORT.)

TOUR A—$13.25.

Phila. Wil. & Balto. R. R...to Phiadelphia
Pennsylvania R. R.........,to New York
Fall River (Sound) Steamers to Fall River
(VIA NEWPORT.)
Old Colony R. R.... ...to New Bedford
Nantucket Steamboat Co. to Oak Bluffs &
[Nantucket
Return by same Route.

———o———

Baltimore to Nantucket
(VIA NEW YORK, NEWPORT & BOSTON)

TOUR B—$14.50.

Same as Route A... ....to Nantucket
Nantucket Steamboat Co...to Woods Hull
Old Colony R R..............to Boston
Old Colony R. R...........to Fall River
Fall River Steamboat.......to New York
Penna. R R. & P W. & B. R. R. to Balto.

———o———

Balto. to White Mountains.
(VIA NEW YORK, NEWPORT & BOSTON.)

TOUR C—$19 50.

P. W. & B R. R ....to Phiadelphia
Penna. R. R...............to New York
Fall River Steamer...to Newport & Boston
Eastern R. R ....to North Conway
Portland & Ogdensburg R.R .to Fabyan's
[White Mountains.
Return by same Route..... .to Baltimore

———o———

Balto. to White Mountains and Mt. Desert.
(VIA NEW YORK, BOSTON & PORTLAND.

TOUR D—$24.50.

Route same as C..............to Fabyans
Portland & Ogdensburg R. R to Portland
Portland, Bangor & Machias Steamboat Co)
[to Mt. Desert
"   "   "   "   to Portland
Eastern R. R.:.................to Boston
Route same as B ....to Baltimore

Baltimore to Mt. Desert
(VIA NEW YORK, BOSTON & PORTLAND.)

TOUR E—$20.50.

Route same as C...............to Boston
Eastern R. R.................to Portland
Portland, Bangor & Machias Steamboat to
[Mt. Desert
"   "   "   "   to Portland
Route same as B........... to Baltimore

———o———

Balto. to White Mountains.
(VIA NEW YORK, NANTUCKET & BOSTON.)

TOUR F—$22.75.

The same as Tour C, adding the trips to Martha's Vineyard and Nantucket.

———o———

Balto. to White Mountains and Mt. Desert.
(VIA NEW YORK, NEWPORT, NANTUCKET AND BOSTON.)

GRAND TOUR G—$28.00,

P. W. & B. R. R........ .to Philadelphia
Penna. R. R ....to New York
Fall River Str. to Newport & Fall River
Old Colony R. R..........to New Bedford
Steamer.....to Oak Bluffs and Nantucket
Steamer..................to Woods Hull
Old Colony R. R......... .. to Boston
Eastern R. R...........to North Conway
Portland & Ogdensburg R. R. to Fabyan's
[White Mountains
"   "   "   to Portland
Portland, Bangor & Machias Steamboat Co.
[to Mt Desert
"   "   "   "   to Portland
Eastern R. R...................to Boston
Fall River Steamer....to New York City
Penna. R. R....... .....to Philadelphia
P. W. & B. R. R...........to Baltimore

PRICE OF TICKETS.

Baltimore to Nantucket and return—Tour A.................................**$13.25.**
Baltimore to Nantucket, Boston and return—Tour B......... **14.50.**
Baltimore to Boston, White Mountains and return—Tour C............... .... **19.50.**
Baltimore to White Mountains, Mt. Desert and return—Tour D............... **24.50.**
Baltimore to Boston, Mt. Desert and return—Tour E..................... **20.50.**
Baltimore to Nantucket, Boston, White Mountains and return—Tour F........ **22.75.**
Baltimore to Nantucket, Boston, White Mts. Mt. Desert—**Grand Tour G..** **28.00.**
Children from 5 to 12 years of age, half fare.

SPECIAL REDUCED RATES

Have been secured from the following points to Baltimore and return, in connection with, these tours. for the benefit of those residing outside of Baltimore. Tickets can be procured at any of the places herewith named, by paying the additonal charge annexed.

Washington, D, C. Baltimore & Potomac R. R & Cor, 13th & Penna, Ave...$2.00
Frederick, Md , B & O. R. R. Office..... .... 2 50
Richmond, Va., A, W. Garber, 826 Main Street............. ....10.50
Hagerstown, Md., West Md. R. R. Office.................................... 2.25
Fredericksburg, Va., Richmond, Fredericksburg & P. R. R. Office........... 6.50
Waynesboro Station, Pa , or Pen-Mar. Ticket Office, West Md. R R. 2.00
York, Pa., Pa. R. R. Office................. .. .. 1 00

Tourists from York, Pa. go via Philadelphia.

Tourists from Wilmington, Del., procure tickets at P. W. & B. R. R. Office, and C. F. Thomas & Co., Stationers, Wilmington.

Tourists from Martinsburg, Va , Greencastle, Chambersburg, Pa., and vicinity, can purchase tickets at Hagerstown, Md.

Special low rates made to Societies, Lodges and Clubs.

For further information not contained in this book, call on or address, *Main Office* Stork's Select Summer Tours, 220 W. Baltimore St., Baltimore

For the information of tourists who have not before visited these localities and to add to the educational features of this trip, short notices of the most interesting points are subjoined, with illustrations, beginning with Newport, R. I. and concluding with interesting sketches of White Mountains and Mt. Desert. Nearly every place referred to here is directly on the line of these Tours.

FALL RIVER LINE OF STEAMERS

BETWEEN NEW YORK AND BOSTON,

(USED ON STORK'S SUMMER TOURS.)

AMERICA'S FLOATING PALACES.

There is no steam line engaged in inland traffic which can boast of having as large and fine a fleet of vessels as the Old Colony Steamship Company. Two of its steamers are the largest in the world; and it is not exaggeration to say that *they are the finest on the globe without any exception.*

THE BRISTOL is 373 feet in length, the hull proper measuring 3,000 tons. The engine has a power equal to 2,800 horses.

PROVISIONS FOR SAFETY.

Scattered through the saloons, are fire-extinguishers; 3 large fire pumps are ready at all times with hose attached, and having 15 connections; fire buckets are distributed in convenient places; large water-tanks are always filled and ready for use. "The Bristol" has 13 life boats, two large life-rafts, and cork mattresses; 700 cork life-belts are now on board, and one is placed in each berth.

SOCIAL HALL.

As we enter the boat and pass the portals of the gangway door, we are ushered into the Social Hall, the flooring of which is black walnut and yellow pine, laid in narrow strips. The ceiling and paneling is in the highest style of the decorator's art. Heavy rosewood doors are on either hand, and rich gas-jets light it up like a fairy grotto. After glancing around for a few minutes, one seems at a loss which way to go, for the beauties of the other parts of the vessel are now revealed, as either the doors leading to the ladies' saloon, or those leading to the grand saloon, are opened by those passing to and fro.

THE LADIES' SALOON.

Velvet carpets, rich and heavy furniture upholstered in velvet and embroidered in chaste patterns, costly chandeliers, and all the appointments of ease, luxury, and refinement, are on every hand. You peep into the staterooms on either side of the saloon and snowy linen, lace curtains and all modern conveniences meet your gaze. Ascending the grand staircase, we are lead into the grandest steamer saloon in the world, 275 feet in length, 28 feet wide, 21 feet high. The staircase is of mahogany, inlaid with satin and other rich woods; and in each of the newel posts is a *petite* chandelier, fit for the boudoir of a nymph.

THE MAIN SALOON.

is nearly 300 feet in length. Elegance, magnitude and superb fittings greet the eyes, which ever way they turn. From the half domed ceiling drop costly chandeliers, in the sunbeams darting forth the bright rays of the trembling prism, or by gaslight sparkling with all the brilliancy of a tiara of diamonds. Soft velvety carpets lush your tread; luxuriant velvet plush-covered lounges, chairs, divans and ottomans invite you to rest.

STATE-ROOMS.

There are 240 state-rooms, including 9 BRIDAL-ROOMS. The latter are furnished with rich carpets, massive bedsteads, dressing-cases, wash-stands, marble top tables and chairs, and are nearly as large as a bedroom in a Fifth Avenue mansion. The upholstery and fittings are magnificent. Each of these rooms is as richly decorated, but several of them are in different colors; so that no "sameness" marks these special chambers.

THE DINING SALOON.

Meals are served on all the boats of this line *a la carte,*—" you order what you want and pay for what you get." The decorations are in keeping with all the other parts of the boat. The silver is massive, the glass chaste, the china appropriate, and everything is inviting and attractive about the place. One of the advantages of this line, is that these boats have a long night trip, and the tourist has a good night's rest in a floating palace.

MUSIC.

A splendid Orchestra of accomplished artists adds its attractions to the pleasures and enjoyments of the trip on the steamers, giving nightly concerts of choice classical and popular music. The two hours of entertainment thus furnished, constitute one of the most enjoyable features of the voyage. When tired with the toils of the day, you have but to seek your state-room, and, locked in the arms of a marine Morpheus, you sleep till the hour of rising is announced.

NAVIGATION.

The officers are *picked men, those who know their duty, and who conscientiously feel their great responsibility.* Perfect system. vigilance, great care and watchfulness are the guiding precepts in every department of the great line. The kind and courteous attention of officers and employees to the comfort of passengers is a remarkable characteristic of the management of these boats and greatly contributes to the satisfaction of the traveler.

CITY OF NEWPORT, R. I.

NEWPORT, R. I.—The first sea-side resort on the line of these tours is, without a rival, *the* fashionable watering-place of America. Its magnificent sea-view, its unsurpassed beach, its drive-ways and boulevards, its private cottages and magnificent public and private dwellings, are not excelled on the Continent. Its hotels have long been famous as the most celebrated in the country.

It is difficult, to decide what constitutes its greatest charm—the delicious climate, the grand old bay, the unequalled location, its long and continuous beaches, or the elegance of its cottages and villas. Approached from the sea in one of the steamers of the Fall River Line, in the early morning, after passing Point Judith, fifteen miles from Newport, Beaver Tail Light House is in view; further up we pass the Dumplings and the old round tower and the beautiful island of Canonicut, and are under the walls of Fort Adams, from which we hear the sound of bugles, and presently the roar of the morning gun. On our left is Goat Island and Fort Wolcott; on our right, Lime Rock, of Ida Lewis fame. Newport offers unrivaled facilities to those who enjoy the whirl of fashionable life at a watering-place; at the same time it offers repose and quiet for those who seek retirement. It will be especially attractive this season on account of the large number of noted people who are expected there, among whom are mentioned, the new Viceroy of Canada, the Marquis of Lorne, and the Marchioness, the Princess Louisa.

Driving is a passion and a pastime in Newport, and nowhere on the Continent are such elegant turnouts to be seen, or the reins handled more dexterously. "The drive" is an institution, and is to be witnessed in the latter part of every pleasant afternoon on Bellevue and Ocean Avenues, and on "Fort days," on the roads to and from the fortress. Bellevue Avenue, between the hours of five and seven P. M., presents one of the gayest scenes im-

THE DRIVE.

aginable. The l orn is heard behind you; you turn—Polo is just over, and down the aye-
nue at a break-neck speed comes t l e coaching club—five magnificent turn-outs, all four-in-
hands—the veritable coaches of olden times of "Merrie England."

At t l eir sides, behind t l em, in front of t l em to the length of t l e avenue in either direction, drawn by t l orough-bred horses—tandems, prancing teams. four and six-in-hands—
are barouches, coupes, dog-carts, landaus, cabriolets, and every form of vehicle known and
unknown—all are pressed into service and lend a clarm to the whirl of life.

On two days in eacl week, t l e gates of Fort Adams are t l rown open; the command-
ant keeps open house, the bands playing at intervals.

CLIFF WALK.

The walks are probably even more sought
after than the drives. Foremost among t l ese is
t l e Cliff Walk along the sea bluffs, on w l ich
t l e pedestrian may continue his rambles to
Easton's Beach and round the southern point
to Fort Adams.

No one w l o visits Newport should fail to
take this Cliff Walk. Certainly, no one who
stands on t l e beach and sees down its long line
the waves breaking against reef and wall,
showering t l e spray like globules of silver in
the sunlight, can resist t l e temptation Although this walk is lined with the finest residences on t l e island—many of them costing
from $25,000 to $500,000 eacl—the ancient rig l t
of fisl ery is still retained, and their banks are
left free to all, and the generosity of t l e owners
of the various estates l as provided a fine, broad
promenade over t l is portion of the island.

While the scene for the entire lengtl of t l e
walk is one to be t l oroughly enjoyed, t l e finest
spot of special interest is Forty Steps, or Con
rad's Cave, at the foot of Narraganset avenue
The steps are a favorite resort and one could
sit for hours of a pleasant day at their foot,
watching t l e heavy swells advancing and retreating, following one another over the rocks
in a lazy, sluggish succession.

The Boat house is at the southern ex-
tremity of the island, just at the foot of Ledge
Road. This is a place famous as the resort of
fisl ermen and for clam bakes. Directly in front
is Coggesl all Ledge, forming a natural break-
water and affording a natural landing.

Furtl er along we come to Bailey's Beach,
and among that mass of rocks piled in wild con-
fusion just across the beach will be found Spouting Rock. T l is is a *cave* into w l ich, t l e
wind and tide being favorable, t l e water
rusl es with a tremendous velocity, and returning is t l rown from
fifty to a hundred feet into t l e air, t l rougl an opening in t l e roof
of the cave. A soutl-east wind and ebbing tide are the requisite
conditions. The most entl usiastic lover of nature will be glad to
take the avenue for town. after a walk around t l e Cliffs

Anotl er fine walk is to Easton's Point, Purgatory Bluffs
and Hanging Rock, or by t l e fort road to t l e fortress T l e visitor
must not fail to spend a few hours on Canonicut Island, crossing
the l arbor by steam ferry. From the old tower on the Dumplings, is one of t l e finest views of Narragansett Bay to be had on its
coast.

Just on the southern end of t l e inner harbor, lie Lime Rocks witl
their friendly lig l t. T l ey have been rendered famous by t l e splendid
acl ievements of Ida Lewis, the Grace Darling of America.

Thousands have visited l er at l er lonely home on the Rocks. Thousands who have not visited her l ave sl owered t l eir letters of respect and
praise upon her. Otl ers l ave manifested their regard by more substan-
tial means. The city of Newport presented l er witl a beautiful boat, t l e
Rescue, and Jim Fisk built a l ouse for it. Resolutions were unanimously
adopted by the General Assembly of t l e State of Rl ode Island, acknowl-

edging her valuable services in saving many lives. She was also presented with a medal costing one hundred dollars. The curious can see Miss Lewis and her medals almost any time at her home on the Rocks.

Whether you visit the cliffs or the shores, or linger around historical spots, you are sure to return. At each visit the scenery grows wilder and more enchanting, until unconsciously you find yourself walking the same paths, looking at the same scenes time upon time, with an admiration and wonder that know no abatement, and you reluctantly leave, murmuring—"The Italy of America."

The climate, too, is most salutary. The heat of the most torrid summer is modified by the cool and refreshing breeze from off the ocean, and the most rigid winter is tempered by the gentle influence of the gulf stream that flows near by.

From the Aquidneck House, on Pelham street, you have a pleasant walk up Pelham to Bellevue avenue, thence along the avenue to Bath Road, turning down this road to the beach.

The beach with its gay costumes, presents all the colors of the kaleidoscope. From the hour of ten till one the scene is lively and interesting. Hundreds in fantastic costumes are plunging into Neptune's cooling element. The shore is lined with vehicles of every description, their occupants watching the bathers or pleasantly chatting the time away. The beach is extremely safe with very little undertow, so that the most timid can venture in.

One of the most remarkable relics of past ages is the old Stone Mill, standing in Touro Park. The origin of this antique structure is a matter of dispute among antiquarians, some claiming it to have been erected by the old Norse Voyagers, and others that they are only the walls of an ancient windmill, built by the contemporaries of the Pilgrim Fathers. It is in the form of a circular tower, resting on eight irregular columns. Present evidence is in favor of the earlier settlers, and against the northmen.

A PLEASANT RIDE.—The Newport Omnibus Co. have a large, English coach which leaves Touro street, Washington Square, near the Perry House, every pleasant afternoon about 2 o'clock, for a drive of nine miles along Bellevue avenue, taking in the Ocean Drive, Bailey's Beach, Spouting Rock, Brenton's Reef, Beaver Tail Light and other interesting points. The driver of this coach is very communicative and makes the drive doubly interesting by his very graphic and pleasing description of the route. Ample time is given passengers to stop at any of the points and ramble through and around the rocks and beach. The charge is only 50 cents, and is well worth the price asked.

Coaches run along Bellevue avenue at intervals of every fifteen minutes. Fare to either of the beaches, Easton's or Bailey's, from Commercial Wharf, 15 cents.

The visit to Newport should be made on the return trip. In going north the steamer does not reach there until about 2 A. M., an inconvenient hour to disembark, while in returning, the tourist can take the Old Colony Railroad at Boston, in the early morning or afternoon, as the tickets are good either by Rail or Steamer, and arrive at Newport in about three hours.

Attention is called to the hotels at this place, herewith advertised. It will be seen that one can spend a few days or weeks at Newport, with first-class entertainment, as economically as at many other less pretentious places.

FALL RIVER,

called the "Border City," because of its situation on the line of Rhode Island, is forty-nine miles from Boston, by rail. It is a manufacturing city—the great New England city of spindles—beautifully located on Mount Hope Bay.

The Tourist will arrive at this point about daylight of the second day of the trip, and if your ticket reads to Martha's Vineyard and Nantucket, you will proceed in the cars of the Old Colony Railroad, (should your ticket read direct to Boston, you take the Boston Express, leaving about half an hour earlier, which going through Taunton, lands you in Boston in two hours,) waiting at the landing, by a delightful ride of 26 miles (via Myrics) to **NEW BEDFORD**, Massachusetts. This ancient city of some 25,000 inhabitants, is well worth seeing, It is situated on the Acushnet river; was settled in 1664 by Quakers. It is built on the side of a ridge sloping to the waters edge. "It has a cosmopolitan air always blowing over its strata." The upper part of the city is pleasant, and County street is lined with stately old residences. It has been called "a city of palaces." These "palaces" are all the model of the "Architectural Boulders" so common in the decadent fishing ports along the coast. The favorite drive is around Clark's Point, which extends into Buzzard's Bay, and is bordered by a broad, smooth road, constructed at great expense by the city, to give its people the benefits of the sea-breezes in summer. This avenue (five miles around) affords a brilliant scene on sultry summer afternoons. Do not fail of a ramble and drive in NEW BEDFORD. The tourist reaches this ancient and interesting city about 7 A. M. on the second day of the tour. The Steamer (either the Island Home or River Queen) is waiting to carry him to Martha's Vineyard and Nantucket, a delightful ride of 25 miles. After passing Wood's Holl, on the left, the sail in the steamer is of itself an epoch in a lifetime,

"The sail across the Sound," says a favorite writer.* "is more than beautiful; it is a poem." Trending away to the west, the Elizabeth Islands, like a gate ajar, half close the entrance to Buzzard's Bay. Among them nestles Cuttyhunk, where the very first English spade was driven into New England soil. Straight over in front of the pathway the steamer is cleaving, the Vineyard is looking its best and greenest, with oak-skirted highlands enclosing the sheltered harbor of Vineyard Haven, famous on all this coast.

MARTHA'S VINEYARD.

The Island of Martha's Vineyard, which is reached at about 8 o'olock A. M., is twenty-one miles in length, and from seven to ten in width. The surface of the land on the eastern portion is mostly level. A range of hills crosses the island from Tisbury Pond on the south to Lombard's Cove on the north and extends to the western shore, terminating in a wild and fantastic cliff one hundred and thirty feet above the sea, at Gay Head, on which is a revolving light. This peculiar headland, the earth and rocks of which are belted with gay colors, from which it received its name, presents a charming picture from the sea, as well as an interesting and wonderful sight on land.

Within the cool groves of Martha's Vineyard, are myriads of cottages of the summer sojourners. Two of the more extensive groves are occupied as camp-grounds by the Methodists and Baptists. Oak Bluffs is a Liliputian city; *within a radius of a mile it has over a thousand cottages*, some of them elegant and costly, owned and occupied by prominent and wealthy citizens from various sections of the country. It has wide avenues for driving, paved with the best concrete, free from mud and dust, and affording grand views of the ocean, a horse-railroad, a trotting course, gas street-lamps, and all modern improvements. As watering-place hotels, some of those on the Vineyard are without superiors.
The entire fleet passing east and west through Vineyard Sound are within sight of nearly all the hotels, bringing into view often a thousand sail. As many as forty thousand visitors have been on the island at one time, in the height of the season.

All the sports and pastimes of a fashionable watering-place are enjoyed. The cottages are tasteful, some of them very elegant; and, at night when illuminated, the whole city has the appearance of a fairy village.

A fine beach road leads to Edgartown, and a narrow-guage steam railroad connects it with "Katama, the Beautiful," and with the South Beach, where the waves dash up against the shore with awful majesty.

At Katama, two or three times a week, there are famous Clam-bakes, and large parties make the trip by these little narrow-guage cars to this lovely spot to dine on the freshly roasted clams and other delicacies.

*Drake, in "Nooks and Corners of New England."

CENTRAL HOUSE

MONTGOMERY SQUARE,

Oak Bluffs, Martha's Vineyard,

BOTH EUROPEAN & AMERICAN PLAN.

CHESTER BALL. so well known last season as the manager of the 'Grover House, at which so many Baltimoreans stopped, has purchased the above Hotel and is now prepared to accommodate guests with rooms with and without meals, or table board alone.

Rooms (Accommodating Two Persons,) $1.00 per Day and Upwards.

Special rates will be offered to Stork's Tourists, and satisfaction guaranteed in every particular.

House open from June 25th to September 15th. The location is a very eligible one, being the centre of all places of interest on the Island.

CHESTER BALL, Proprietor.

COTTAGE LIFE AT THE VINEYARD.

SEA BATHING.

The beach at Oak Bluffs is one of the finest in the world. It is plentifully supplied with neat bathing-houses, which are kept clean and in good repair. In the centre of the plank promenade which skirts the "bluffs" is a picturesque pavilion where those who do not wish to "tempt the waves" may witness the sport at a safe distance. At about 11 o'clock A. M. each day, a sight may here be enjoyed, such as is seen nowhere else in the country. From 500 to 1000 or more people take their daily plunge in old ocean. There is ordinarily but little surf at this point and absolutely no under tow whatever, so that the most timid ladies, who cannot be induced to go in at other places, soon gather confidence and splash about with liveliest enjoyment and enthusiasm. Many of the bathing-dresses are made after the French modes and are quite elaborate and ornamental. Instead of transforming the wearer into a fright they are tasteful and becoming. The slouts of the bathers, the beauty of the beach, the playful splashing of the waves, the passing fleet of white-winged ships in the offing and the gay concourse of beauty and fashion which lines the bluffs and crowd the pavilion, contribute to make a spectacle never to be forgotten.

"THE BLUFFS."

One of the greatest attractions of Martha's Vineyard, is the ocean promenade at Oak Bluffs. It is a wide plank walk skirting the edge of the bluffs for a mile or more. On pleasant days and nights this is thronged with pedestrians and is the favorite resort of young ladies and gentlemen for a romantic walk and quiet talk. On a moonlight night the scene from the bluffs is entrancing. The sheen of the moon, on the wide waters, the graceful ships, the music of the waves and the back-ground of handsome cottages, give the impression of a delightful dream. What wonder that this place should be famous for love-making and flirtatious which are here popularly known as "bluffing."

The Grand Illumination at Martha's Vineyard about August 24th, is a most brilliant spectacle, rivaling the great fetes of Vienna and Paris. This is a gala day on the Island, and is witnessed every year by people from all parts of the country. Tourists of the August Series of Tours can participate in this Illumination.

NANTUCKET.—From Oak Bluffs to Nantucket is a delightful sail. The approach to the island is a joy and a surprise. The island of Nantucket is a crescent, of which the two horns project far to the north-west. The town of Nantucket lies on the inner face of the cresent, protected from the violence of the ocean's waves by these two natural breakwaters. The sail of about thirty-seven miles consumes a little more than three hours, and a part of the time you are almost out of sight of land. At last

NANTUCKET, FROM THE CHURCH TOWER.

the white spires of the town begin to show themselves on the horizon, while the great projections on the right and left, like gigantic arms, seem to extend to one the embrace of that hospitality for which the island is justly famous. Gradually the houses, rising one above another, come distinctly in view. The steamer rounding the light-house on Brant Point, draws up at one of the four or five wharves upon which the active commerce of the place once displayed itself. Varied as is the assemblage that gathers on the wharf are the carriages that stand ready for reception of any stray passenger. There is the unavoidable hack of course, to accommodate the fashionable visitor and carry him to one or the other of the hotels; and a few carry-alls of foreign construction. But the majority of the vehicles are those peculiar wagons which the old-fashioned Nan-tucketer clings to with fond affection and styles his *carts*. The more modern cart has four wheels, and resembles an ordinary coal wagon.

Nantucket harbor extends some three miles inland in a northeasterly direction from the town, terminating in a basin about one mile in width, known as the Head of the Harbor, and affording pleasant boating and sailing to those who prefer smooth waters to the dashing billows outside. A small steamer, and Sail Boats make regular trips between the town and the Head of the Harbor, touching at Wauwinet, a small village whose Indian name would be very expressive if meaning, "*a place for a dinner*." Here can be obtained a regular Fish Dinner—fresh from the ocean. Nantucket, with its invigorating sea air and quiet repose offers strong attractions to the invalid, while it invites all to its recreations and rest from activities of city life.

Nantucket has her hotels, large and commodious, whose charges are moderate, and ac-commodations homelike. Besides the hotels and boarding-houses, there are many families who are prepared to receive boarders for the season or for a visit.

The appearance of the town itself is very singular. The houses, especially in the south-ern part, rise one above the other, somewhat after the fashion of Quebec. The shingled sides and small paned windows are sufficient marks of their age. The most palpable relic of the time of the whale-fishery, however, is found in the many "*walks*," as they are styled, which are even yet preserved. Of old no whale-fisherman thought of inhabi-ting a house from whose roof he could not obtain an easy and pleasant out-look upon the harbor, or at least gather some idea of the prospects of the weather, and the prob-able return of the sailing craft of the place. The platform is small or large, built around a single chimney and barely accommodating two or three persons at a time, or running the entire length of the roof, and with room for the whole family to congregate on a pleasant evening; and the balustrade surrounding it is as plain or as ornamental as the taste or means of the occupant may have dictated.

A slort distance from the town tle eye takes in tle principal bathing ground, wlose growing attractions draw strangers hitler from all parts of tle country. Safety, quiet and delicious temperature, such are its characteristics and nowhere can tlese be found in greater perfection. Tlose who love the rough surf need but to drive three miles to the southern side of the island, or to take up tleir abode in tle fishing village at its eastern end; but the majority who shun the perils of the "under tow" can ask for nothing better than what they can find just out of town at tle Cliffs, wlither a fast sailing pleasure sloop is constantly in readiness to take them.

The *Windmills* of Nantucket are quite an interesting feature. which, in the total absence of water power, lave from time immemorial ground all the corn the island produces.

A drive or a walk to Surfside, on tle soutl slore, about two and a half miles by tle road leading near tle old mill, and an hour on tle beach with the rolling surf at our feet, is a part of the programme wlicl we cannot afford to omit. Nor is a visit to The Cliffs, on the north shore, less interesting. Here numerous summer residences overlook the bay, and batling-houses skirt the beach affording ample opportunities for bathing on one of the finest beaches on the island. Conveyances to the Cliffs, either by water or land are ample and inexpensive. To the wayfarer it is only a pleasant walk of about one mile from town.

One of the first excursions you make should be to tle small village of Siasconset, commouly abbreviated into "*Sconset.*" The ride thither is one of seven or eight miles. The village las quite merged its character of a fishing village into that of a watering-place. The rude cottages have been modified so as to accommodate the new visitors, and numbers of houses in the town of Nantucket have been taken down and removed to Siasconset.

BLUE-FISHING.

For whicl Nantucket is so famous, may be enjoyed on the beach on the south shore of the island by the "heave and haul" method, which is simply casting a line among tle breakers, and hauling it in quickly. This requires practice to "get the hang of it," To enjoy blue fishing, however, to its fullest extent, it is desirable to commit yourself to an experienced "skipper," of which there is no scarcity. If we go "for the fun of the thing," we want a company of some half a-dozen; but if our aim is to catch fish, the number may be limited as fancy or circumstances dictate. Once on the "ground," one's attention is wholly absorbed in the excitement incident to the sport. The boatmen may perlaps steer along the northwestern shore for Great Point; or, if not succesful here, will "double the cape" and run along the eastern side of the island. Some of these localities, if not all, are pretty sure of giving tle sportsman ample employment. Another noted fishing-gronnd is tle "Opening," a channel between the western part of Nantucket and a small island named Tuckauuck. If accustomed to blue fisling, one only needs his experience and lis hook and line to bring them on board; but, if it is a first attempt, it may be a little difficult to keep cool. Experience, however, will soon render one calm, after which success is certain.

The insular character of Nantucket, and its comparative distance from the mainland, have conferred upon its natives a number of peculiarities tlat render society here quite different from almost anywhere else. The Coffins, the Folgers, the Starbucks, tle Macys, the Barnards, tle Swains are each to be counted by hundreds. By intermarriages almost the entire island is bound together. The interests of all are the same and their tastes similar. The summer visitor has little conception of tle seclusion of Nantucket in winter. Even now, it often happens tlat all communication with the mainland is cut off by stormy weather for a week or ten days.

It was not until 1765 tlat tle supply of whales in the immediate vicinity grew so small that the practice of going out from tle slore to pursue tlem was entirely abandoned. Meanwhile, however, the enterprise of the islanders had been aroused, and ships were built to cruise in search of the retreating prey. By the middle of the century the Nantucket whalemen lad penetrated Davis's Straits and Baffin's Bay. Not rarely a ship well equipped, and furnished witl the greatest care, met with sucl reverses tlat after being absent tlree or four years, sle returned only to exhibit a consderable positive loss of money to her owners. officers and men, each one of whom took a certain proportionate interest in the undertaking. The largest sum we have heard of a single voyage netting was $108,000, of which about two-thirds went to tle owners.

Hotels & Boarding Houses.—Nantucket, Mass.

NAME.	PER DAY.
OCEAN HOUSE—Head of Broad Street,	$2.50 to $3.00
R. P. FOLGER—No. 7 Fair Street,	$1.25
MRS. A. M. ENAS—Union Street	1.25
CAPT. T. G. NICKERSON—Next to Springfield House	1.25
MRS. W. H. MYRICK—N. Water Street	1.25
MRS. FISH—Broad and N. Water Streets.	1.50
CAPT. DAVIS—147 Orange Street,	1.00
VALENTINE O. HOLMES—Main and Federal Streets	1.25
MRS. L. C. HOLWAY—Broad Street, opposite Ocean House	1.00
MRS. WAITTE,—No. 9 Pearl Street.	1.25

NANTUCKET TO BOSTON.

Tourists returning from Nantucket to Baltimore direct, return by same route, via Martha's Vineyard and New Bedford. Those returning via Boston, take steamer from Nantucket to the Vineyard, thence to Wood's Holl, taking cars at the latter place by Old Colony Railroad. The first important place reached is

FALMOUTH

A quiet place of rest and recreation. Situated on a promontory forming the extreme southern point of the town is Woods Holl—the southern terminus of this branch of the Old Colony R. R. From Nobska Hill we have a charming view of the Sound, of the Vineyard shore, of Tisbury Hills, and of the Elizabeth Islands. From the same stand-point, looking northward across the neck of land, the whole stretch of Buzzard's Bay is before us.

FALMOUTH HEIGHTS.,

One of the most delightful resorts bordering on Vineyard Sound, reached by carriage from Falmouth Station, on the Old Colony Railroad. Here we find a fashionable watering-place, combined with a delightful and inexpensive retreat for a summer's sojourn, a week's recreation, or a day's pastime. The next Summer Resort is

COHASSETT NARROWS,

Separating Wareham from Sandwich, is a connecting strait between Buzzard's Bay and Buttermilk Bay and is one of the best among the many localities in this section for blue fish tautog, sea trout, bass, etc. And near the road, the tourist has an almost uninterrupted view during the whole ride to Woods Holl,—a panorama of singular beauty, embracing some of the cosiest nooks and corners of the whole southern coast of Massachusetts,—nooks that are rapidly filling with the neat cottages of the summer residents,—the gentle sweep of the westerly breezes up the magnificent bay, with the protection of the cape on the northerly side, rendering the climate delightful.

WAREHAM,

49 miles from Boston,—celebrated for its numerous ponds and streams. Passing through Middleboro, we glide swiftly through a succession of beautiful towns and villages and shortly reach the great city of Boston.

THE CITY OF BOSTON the metropolis of New England, is one of the most ancient and famous of American Cities. In spite of its great fires and rapid changes, Boston has more of a European appearance than any other American city. It has also a distinguished aristocracy of old families, and the intellectual and musical culture of its citizens is world renowned.

The historic Associations connected with Boston, its Libraries and Museums, its elegant stores and palatial residences, together with its picturesque suburban scenery, render it one of the most interesting cities to visit on the continent. Besides this the many delightful places within easy reach and to which short excursions can be made by land or water, add greatly to its attractions. For the benefit of those who are not familiar with the city, we herewith give a list of some of its most important objects of interest.

FANEUIL HALL, the "Cradle of American Liberty," is perhaps next to Independence Hall in Philadelphia, the most historically famous building outside of Washington.

The OLD STATE HOUSE, is an ancient landmark, having been built in 1748 and long used by the legislature of Massachusetts, Bay Colony. Fronting on School St. is the CITY HALL, containing the Council Chambers. Corner Washington and Milk Sts., stands the famous OLD SOUTH CHURCH, the 'Shrine of Boston." Corner of Tremont and Boylston Streets, facing the commons is the MASONIC TEMPLE, built in 1864-7, on opposite corners are the hotels Boylston and Pelham, of striking architecture and close at hand is the PUBLIC LIBRARY, in a fire proof building of brick and sandstone. This Library contains 300,000 volumes and 100,000 pamphlets and is the LARGEST IN AMERICA, except the library of Congress, It is open to the public, free to all, but only residents of the city can take books from the building. Corner Park and Tremont Street is the PARK ST. CHURCH, an old puritan meeting house the "citadel and strong hold of orthodoxy," opposite is the famous BOSTON MUSIC HALL, with its great organ which cost $60,000 and further along HORTICULTURAL HALL and TREMONT TEMPLE, in the large hall of which Joseph Cook's great lectures are delivered, and next on the same side of the street comes KING'S CHAPEL, an Episcopal Church built in 1754.

At corner of Tremont and Eliot Streets, is the Y. M. C. A. BUILDING, with Library and Gymnasium, Parlor and Reading Rooms, the latter always open to strangers. On Tremont near School Street the BOSTON MUSEUM, (admission 30 cents.) full of curiosities from all parts of the world. One of most interesting features is BOSTON COMMON. containing 48 acres and situated right in the heart of the city. It has fine lawns and noble trees, a frog pond, with a large fountain supplied from Cochituate Lake. It is ornamented with Brewer Fountain cast in Paris, and one of the most magnificent in the world, and also the Soldiers Monument on Flag Staff Hill. The PUBLIC GARDENS, lie west of the common and contain 22 acres; in the centre is a beautiful serpentine pond of 4 acres crossed by a picturesque bridge, and at different points are a bronze STATUE OF EVERETT, by Story, A MONUMENT TO THE DISCOVERY OF ANÆSTHETICS, VENUS RISING FROM THE SEA, and the magnificent colossal equestrian STATUE OF WASHINGTON, fronting on Commonwealth avenue.

The MUSEUM OF NATURAL HISTORY, corner of Boylston and Berkeley streets, is open to the public on Wednesdays and Saturdays. In the same square is the MASSACHUSETTS INSTITUTE OF TECHNOLOGY, which has 38 professors and nearly 300 students.

At the corner of Huntingdon Avenue and Clarendon street is the new TRINITY (Episcopal) CHURCH—Phillips Brooks, rector—an immense structure of Roxbury stone, which cost over $700,000. No one should fail to visit it.

The MUSEUM OF FINE ARTS is on Art Square, Dartmouth street and Huntingdon avenue. It is worth a trip to Boston to see this magnificent building and examine the wonderful and invaluable collection of pictures, statuary, ceramics, etc , etc. On two days of the week admission is free. At other times 25 cents is charged.

The STATE HOUSE is on the summit of Beacon Hill, fronting the Commons. From its dome, one of the finest views of the city can be obtained. Near the State House, on Beacon street, is the ATHÆNUM, with its reading room and valuable and extensive library.

The Roman Catholic CATHEDRAL of the HOLY CROSS, at the corner of Washington and Malden streets, covers more than an acre of ground, and is one of the longest and highest Cathedrals in the world.

In the extent and beauty of its suburbs Boston may challenge comparison with almost any city in the world. This undulating region dotted with crystal ponds, superbly wooded and covered for miles with country seats, in every conceivable style of architecture, from the Grecian temple to the Mansard roof, is a panorama of delicious pictures.

These suburbs comprise among other interesting places, CAMBRIDGE the seat of the great HARVARD UNIVERSITY with its Collegiate buildings and Memorial Hall. Here is still standing the tree under which Geo. Washington took command of the American army.

DORCHESTER, containing some palatial residences, surrounded by rich grounds and adorned with every variety of ornamental plants and flowers.

CHARLESTOWN, with its famous Bunker Hill Monument.

No one who visits Boston can afford to leave without spending an hour or more in Mt. Auburn Cemetery.

EVERY TOURIST AND TRAVELER

SHOULD HAVE THE

American Plant Book!

BY

Harlan H. Ballard and S. Proctor Thayer,

FOR THE PRESERVATION OF

PRESSED FLOWERS,
FERNS, GRASSES,
FOREST LEAVES, ETC.

PPENDED are leaves of adhesive paper, ruled as a guide for cutting to necessary sizes. A representation of the POISON IVY and SUMACH preceeds the title page, which is followed by full directions for gathering, pressing and mounting specimens. Bound in extra cloth and gilt, with inside pocket.

FOR FOREST LEAVES.
Size 6½x8¾ incles, witl Descriptive Page.
each

No. 1, 56 leaves, extra cloth and gold,.................. ....$1.00
No. 4, 56 leaves, full Russia, rich finish.. 2.00

SCHOOL EDITION.
Size 8¾x11¼ incles. witl Index and Analysis page.

No. 5, 64 leaves, full cloth, stamped..$1.50
No. 8, 64 leaves, full Russia, rich finish,...... ... . 3.50

AMATEUR'S EDITION.
Size, 8¾x11¼, incles, witl Descriptive page.

No. 10, 64 leaves, extra cloth and gold.................··...........................$1.75
No. 14, 64 leaves, full Russia, rich finish... 3.50

STUDENTS' EDITION.
Size, 10x12¾ incles, with Index and Analysis page.

No. 15, 80 leaves, extra cloth and gold...$3.25
No. 18, 80 leaves, full Russia, rich finish.. 5.00

GUMMED HERBARIA PAPER,
Twelve sheets, size 8½x11 inches, per package........ ....25 cts.

"I trust tlat your books may be a source of intelligent delight to many a young person, and in the end a means of storing up tlousands of recollections of pleasant loliday trips and excursions, through bosky brakes or deep forests, over meadow and mountain, or perhaps even of lauglable misadventures on briery lillside, or in treaclerous swamp."

EDWARD H. DAY, Prof. Natural Science,
Normal College, New York City.

Copies sent prepaid by mail or express on receipt of price. For sale by all leading Booksellers and Stationers, and by

STORK, PHIPPS & CO.

AT THEIR NEW STORE,

220 W. Baltimore St., Baltimore.

MRS. S. E. FROST'S BOARDING-HOUSE

No. 15 Joy Street, Boston.

Terms $1.50 per Day. A delightful situation, excellent Table and Cheerful rooms Take South Boston Street-cars at Old Colony Depot, get out corner Park and Tremont streets, walk up Park St. to Mt. Vernon, and thence to Joy St.

MRS. MOORE'S BOARDING-HOUSE.

No. 3 Boylston Place, Boston.

South Boston Cars and Blue Cars marked "Depots" &c. from Old Colony Depot take you to corner Tremont and Boylston streets, one square from Boylston Place. Highly recommended to all tourists Many Baltimoreans were guests at this house last season. **Terms, $1.50 per Day.**

BOSTON TO WHITE MOUNTAINS. There are several routes, from Boston to the White Mountains. The one selected for these tours is via. the Eastern R. R. and is by far the most desirable, being much the shortest and most direct and the only Sea Shore Line. It is delightfully cool in summer as it skirts the ocean a good portion of the way. For safety and comfort and for excellent management it has few superiors and is the only really all-rail line, which runs through the White Mountains without change. The train leaves E R. R. Depot, in Boston and passes out over the Charles River bridge. The heights of Charlestown, crowned by the Bunker Hill Monument, rise on the right and the manufactories of east Cambridge, are seen on the left. The Chelsea Creek and Sawyer's River are crossed and Lynn is soon in sight. This is the great shoe manufacturing city of New England, and contains a population of about 30,000. Soon after leaving Lynn the train reaches Swampscott, a fashionable watering-place, which, like Nahant, is much affected by the aristocracy of Boston. Next comes Salem, the mother city of the Massachusetts Colony, and once the theatre of the famous witchcraft delusion and excitement. It is situated on a long peninsula, between two inlets of the sea,—population about 25,000. In Harmony Grove Cemetery, Geo. Peabody, who founded and endowed our Baltimore Peabody Institute, is buried, and two miles from here is the town of Peabody where he was born. After leaving Salem the road passes through a tunnel 600 feet long and crosses North River on a long bridge, near which a fleet of yachts is generally anchored, and touching at Beverly and Wenham crosses Ipswich river and stops at Ipswich, and soon reaches the ancient and beautifully situated Sea city of Newburyport, where Geo. Whitefield preached and died, and where until his recent death, was the home of Caleb Cushing, the eminent lawyer and diplomatist. Leaving Newburyport the train crosses the Merrimac river on a costly new bridge, affording fine views to the right of the city and river, with the ocean in the distance, and passes over long salt meadows, on the east of which are Hampton Beach and the ocean. From North Hampton Station, stages run four miles to the famous and fashionable watering-place, RYE BEACH, which has become so popular as a select seaside resort, and boasts several noted and elegant hotels.

PORTSMOUTH, the Capitol of New Hampshire and its only seaport, is soon reached, and is a quaint and pleasant old city of 9000 inhabitants, and the birth-place of James T. Fields, Thos. Bailey Aldrich, "Mrs. Partington" and other literate. Here is the great U. S. Navy Yard, with its immense slip houses, machine shops, wharves and dry docks. From Portsmouth the staunch steam yacht "Appledore" runs to the ISLES OF SHOALS, a favorite summer resort, especially for artists and literary people. They consist of eight rocky Islets in the ocean, ten miles from land, and are extremely wild and romantic. Appledore House on Appledore Island and Oceanic Hotel on Star Island, are large, first-class hotels. Beyond Portsmouth the train crosses Piscataqua river, and speeds on to Conway Junction. Here tourists bound for the White Mountains *direct* enter upon the North Conway Division of the Eastern Railroad, while those for Mt. Desert are taken on to Portland by the main stem. The White Mountain train touches at Rochester, Milton, Wakefield, Ossipee, Madison, Conway, and five miles further north, after crossing Saco river, a picturesque village is seen nestling on the hillside, the tower of the Kearsarge House is approached on the right, and the train stops at the new and elegant station building at NORTH CONWAY. Here passengers can take one of the fine Observation Cars of the Portland and Ogdensburg Railroad through the White Mountain Notch. This style of car, a novelty in mountain travel, introduced by the P. & O. R. R., is built like the ordinary passenger car except that the sides are entirely open above the rail. They are fitted with comfortable swivel arm-chairs, and the open sides afford extensive and unobstructed views of the magnificent scenery of this famous mountain pass.

NORTH CONWAY. This village lies on a fertile upland, surrounded by hills and mountains, and overlooking the reaches of the Saco, at the head of which, apparently, is Mt Washington, a monarch among the regiment of giant forms which cluster about it. To the east is a range of hills, with Mt. Kearsarge predominant and to the west of the river is Moat Mountain and the Peaks of Chocorua. These four mountains are the most noticeable, but many others loom up in the north, mantled with depths of purple, blue and gold in the changing light of the day. They are beautiful at all times—beautiful with a beauty of their own that is incomparable to any thing in the Alleghanies or the Rocky mountains.

The neighborhood of Conway contains many natural features of interest, including the Artist's Fall, a picturesque cascade set among forest trees and rocks, and Echo Lake, at the foot of White Horse Ledge. The "White Horse," which can be seen from the village, is the figure of a horse impressed upon the perpendicular side of a range of cliff, which extends four or five miles along the banks of the river, and varies in height from a hundred to eight hundred feet   At one point a natural cavity, called the Cathedral, has been formed in the solid granite, with walls about eighty feet high, and an arched roof. Another picturesque spot is that which is romantically called Dina1's Bath, this is a little farther north than the Cathedral, and is reached by a shady woodland path leading over some granite ledges to a rivulet, which trickles and breaks in silver and white until it tumbles over another ledge about ten feet high, The action of the water has worn several basins in the rocks, the largest being about nine feet in diameter, and the pools thus formed are indeed fit for as chaste a goddess as Diana

At North Conway which is both a rendezvous and a starting point for all explorers of the mountains, the social characteristics are not less interesting than the topography. The society is so select, the accommodations so excellent, the air so invigorating and the scenery so grand that the traveler will be loathe to leave it. The police young gentleman who attends to your wants at table, bringing you a dish of fresh eggs and a glass of creamy milk, if they have been in your order, is a Sophomore at Harvard, and he is not the victim of any bitter reverse in life, as you may be inclined to think. The servants at many of the hotels are college students, who by service of this kind, are enabled to pay their fees ; and the girls in attendance—modest New England girls, with honest intelligent faces and neatly braided hair—are likewise students.

Situated at the gate of the White Mountains. Will open June 15th, and continue under the management of the subscribers. Liberal arrangements made with permanent boarders.

The most beautiful and convenient point around the White Mountains for a long or short stay.

S. W. & S. D. THOMPSON.

Special rate to Stork's Tourists of $2.50 per day.

As we leave Conway we get another view of Mt Kearsarge, which may be ascended by a bridle-path, and our next hostelry is the Crawford House, which is reached through the famous White Mountain Notch. The valley gradually narrows and the hills inclosing it become more abrupt as we travel northward. Rounding Heart's Ledge, the road now turns to the north and crosses Sawyer's river. Soon after Nancy's Brook is crossed by a bridge over a remarkable ravine, after passing the Mt. Crawford House, with Mts. Crawford and Resolution and the Giant's Stairs on the right, the forest closes in on the road which crosses the Saco near the foot of the Giant's Stairs and recrosses it almost a mile beyond, with a fine view of the long deep gorge to the right. We now enter the Notch

THE NOTCH,

with Mt. Webster towering 4000 feet on the right and Willey Mount on the left. Passing the Willey House the road ascends slowly for three miles and passes through the narrow gate of the notch, and stops at the Crawford House. This is a large and elegant summer hotel, with accommodations for 350 guests. The view down the Notch is wonderful; embracing two Titanic mountain walls, beginning with Webster on the left and Willey on the right, and running south for leagues, with haughty Chocurua closing the vista. Bayard Taylor says of this view, "As a sample picture of a mountain pass, seen from above, it cannot be surpassed in all Switzerland.

Silver Cascade, on the left of the Notch Road, is one of the most beautiful falls in the mountains. It descends 1000 feet in 1 mile. The Fabyan House is soon reached; it is an imposing structure, built on the Giant's Grave, a tall mound near the Ammonoosuc river, and can accommodate 500 guests. The view from this point is very fine. This is the ultimate point of our WHITE MOUNTAIN TOUR.—From this place excursions can be made via. Rail to the summit of Mt. Washington, which is in full view, or to the Twin Mountain House, Bethlehem and Littleton. A new railroad is just completed and opened this summer to the Profile House, Echo Lake and the Flume in the Franconia range. This makes a delightful side-trip and will amply repay a visit One making it should stop at the Profile House, which is situated in a region of wonders. In the woods to the north of the hotel is the beautiful Echo Lake, which is of great depth and transparency, and is surrounded by densely wooded hills. A voice, a bugle blast, or a sound of any kind, is repeated from hill to hill with such marvelous distinctness and sweetness of intonation that Tennyson's exquisite lines are at once recalled to the listener's memory:

> "O lark, O lear! how thin and clear,
> And thinner, clearer, farther going!
> O sweet and far from cliff and scar,
> The horns of Elfland faintly blowing!
> Blow, let us hear the purple glens replying:
> Blow, bugle; answer echo, dying, dying, dying."

Overhanging the hotel almost on the north is Eagle Cliff, an immense columnar crag separated from the crest of the mountain, and apparently held by a thread; as you walk down the road to the south of the hotel, a guide-board with the simple legend "Profile" painted upon it indicates that you are approaching the strange conformation of rocks. Profile Rock, which is really fashioned after the head of an old man, and the truth of the likeness makes it a most interesting sight.

ASCENT OF MOUNT WASHINGTON.

From the Fabyan House there are three ways of doing this —by the railroad, (2 trains daily each way,) the carriage road, or afoot. The railway might have suggested Jules Verne's *Journey to the Moon*, and is such a miracle of engineering that it will be a pity if any visitor to the mountains misses a ride over it. The route follows the Ammonoosuc Valley, and from the Fabyan House to the end of the friction rail is six and two-third miles For two and a half miles the grade is one foot of perpendicular height to eighteen feet of horizontal distance. Besides the usual rails, there is a central rail of peculiar construction to receive the motive power, consisting of two bars of iron, with connecting cross-pieces placed four inches apart. A central cog-wheel on the locomotive plays into this rail, and secures a sure and steady mode of ascent and descent.

The locomotive is not connected with the car, but simply pushes it up the ascent and allows it to follow gently in the descent A wrought-iron dog constantly plays into notches on the driving-wheel, so that should any part of the machinery give way, the train may be immediately stopped. The car is also supplied with friction and atmospheric brakes. The seats are placed at an angle that brings them almost on a level in the ascent, and all of them face down the mountain. The time occupied on the journey up is about an hour and a half, the fare, is three dollars up the mountain, three dollars down, or four dollars up and down on the same train. The railway has by no means superseded the carriage road, which is still a favorite route to the summit of the mountain. For the first four miles it winds among a dense growth of forest trees, and thence passes through a ravine, and over the eastern side of the mountain. From the highest of the Rocky Mountains the view unfolded resembles a desolate ocean; from the White Mountains it is an earthly paradise.

Mount Washington, which is 6,293 feet, or nearly a mile and a quarter high, rises over 500 feet above the loftiest of the surrounding peaks.

We have exhausted our space, and yet we have not exhausted our subject; for to even enumerate all the "points of interest" in the White Mountains would make a large book. The angler, the lover of nature, or the prosaic business man can each find a tranquil charm in this region which will make the granite fastnesses of New Hampshire memorable to him for a lifetime.

FABYANS TO NORTH CONWAY AND PORTLAND.
RETURN TRIP.

Tourists can leave Fabyans about 2 P. M., returning by same route through Crawford Notch, a distance of twenty-eight miles The entire route is over the Portland and Ogdensburg Railroad. The mountain views in front and to the left are remarkably fine as you near FRYEBURG. This town is a pretty village, on a broad level plain; quite a comfortable hotel is here and many summer visitors, during the hot months. The train now passes on rapidly through Brownfield, we now near Hiram Bridge; occasional glimpses are caught of Mt. Pleasant. The great falls of the Saco are seen from the train between W. Baldwin and

Hiram Bridge. Passing through W. Baldwin, Baldwin and Steep Falls, we reach SEBAGO LAKE STATION.

This lake is one of the most picturesque in New England; it is 14 miles long and 11 wide—in some parts it is 400 feet deep. Six towns are on its shores. Fine steamers leave Pavilion Bay (at Lake Sebago Station) and sail to Harrison, a small hamlet at the end of the route. The scenery on this beautiful sleet of water is much of it, very wild and rugged.— We think it would amply repay our tourists to stop off and take this pleasant side trip. Our next important stopping place is the city of Portland.

PORTLAND, the Commercial metropolis of Maine, is built on a high peninsula at the south-west end of Casco Bay. Its harbor is deep and well sheltered and defended by three powerful forts. It is a beautiful and prosperous place especially attractive in summer for its coolness, and is popularly called the "Forest City," on account of its large number of beautiful shade trees, The St. Julian Hotel is one of the best on the European plan, Rooms $1.00 per day. The Falmouth Hotel, is the finest in the city, Rates $2.50 and $3.00 per day.

Once more we walk up the gang-plank and step on board one of the fine steamers of the Portland, Bangor and Machias Steamboat Company. It is about 10 o'clock evening, gradually we move off from the wharf out into the grand harbor of Portland.

The accommodations on these steamers are first-class being noted for the excellence of the table, equal to any Hotel. The first landing after leaving Portland, is at Rockland on the Penobscot Bay, which is reached almost before sunrise. The sight of the sunrise on the Camden Hills is with the early rising, these hills are in reality a scene of mountain ranges.

From Rockland the steamer moves on a north-easterly direction leading through the islands that form the town of Islesborough northward and eastward to Castine. This trip of 110 miles is one of the most enjoyable of the entire tour. "Sheltered by outlying islands from the roll of the sea, the route passes many a picturesque inlet and seaside hamlet.— Broad harvest fields, alternate with wooded craig and ledge. The village churches show their spires afar, and the light-houses shine upon the headlands. From Castine you pass Cape Rosier, through the Eggemogin Reach, which is like a broad river, varying in width from one to three miles. Emerging from the Reach and passing the light-house on Harlin Island, the Isle of Haut slows far seaward, on the right, the hill 600 feet high which gave it its name. Now we see the well-wooded slope of the Western mountain in Mount Desert Island. To the left is the Western mountain, then Beach mountain, Dog mountain and Robinson's. Next, on the east, is Brown mountain, now loom up the slopes of Green mountain (1 522 feet high—the highest on the Island) with the little cottage at the top, and the ridge of Newport just seen against the sky beyond.

The first landing on the Island is at South-west Harbor, in the town of Tremont. After leaving South-west Harbor the western hills recede, and the remarkable inlet called Some's Sound appears. Along these shores we find no beach, no sand or marshes. The Atlantic beats against solid walls of rock, and there are a number of bays and inlets, among which cottages and farms lie.—There are numerous small rocky, barren islands on the other side, whose only inhabitants seem to be sea-fowl.

Now we pass "other cliffs". A mile or so further, the great cleft known as Thunder Hole; the Newport Beach, and next that of the frowning bluff of Great Head; here the massive cliffs lift their bold front high in air, as if to challenge the wildest, most furious assaults of wind and wave. Newport mountain now hides all the others with its steep and rugged cliffs. Now and then there is a glimpse of the Schooner-Head road. The head itself cannot be mistaken on account of the likeness in front of a fore-and-aft schooner, with jib and mainsail set.—Below it, at low tide, can be seen the opening into the chasm of the "Spouting Horn." Across the Cove, at low tide, also, the dark mouth of the "oven" is visible. The pretty cottages at "Shooner Head" warn the traveler that "Bar Harbor," our destination and the end of the tour, is near at hand. The entrance to Bar Harbor is very charming, and although you have been enchanted by the picturesque and thoroughly delightful sail along the shores of the Island, the enchantment is not broken by the end of the voyage. Hotels and cottages are scattered about, the Island looks green and fresh, the waters are dotted with sail and row-boats, and the impression one gets is that he is far removed from the busy haunts of men, and that all there is to do is to enjoy himself. The hotel accommodations are ample and very good.

MOUNT DESERT is an Island 14 miles long and 8 wide at its greatest breadth, and is distinguished for its wild and romantic scenery of mountain, lake and shore. It is said there is no other point on the Atlantic coast of North America where such magnificent scenery is found; the sublimity of the mountains challenging the eternal grandeur of the sea. There are 13 distinct mountain peaks, with numerous lakes, and a deep, narrow arm of the sea runs to the north through the island. The view from the village of BAR HARBOR is very pretty, extending across Porcupine Islands, in Frenchman's Bay, to the hills of Goldsborough. Near the village are beaches, and near by, on a high rocky islet, is the summer residence of Gen. Fremont. Among other points of interest on the Island. are the following :

CROMWELL'S COVE about 1½ miles south of BAR HARBOR, on the bold rocky shores of which is seen the rock figure called "The Assyrian," the "Indian's Foot"—a print in the rock, and "The Pulpit," are in this vicinity.

SCHOONER HEAD, 4 miles south of BAR HARBOR, by a road leading under Newport mountain on the right, and with the bay and the round-backed and bristling Porcupine Islands on the left. It is a high wave-washed cliff, with a white place on its seaward side which resembles a schooner under sail. Near by is the SPOUTING HORN and Mermaid's Cave, and 1½ miles further is GREAT HEAD, the highest headland between Cape Cod and New Brunswick, with wonderful Cliffs and Chasms and a broad view of the ocean.

NEWPORT BEACH stretches beyond Great Head to Thunder Cave, (entered only by boat) which is in the lofty Otter Creek Cliffs,

JORDAN'S POND is 9 miles south-west of BAR BARBOR, by a road passing through Echo Notch, and affords fine trout fishing, as does also EAGLE LAKE, 2½ miles west of Bar Harbor, and reached by a path leaving the road near Green mountain.

GREEN MOUNTAIN is near Bar Harbor, from which a road runs 4 miles to the summit, where there is a small hotel where accommodations for the night may be obtained. The view from Green mountain is marvelous. No other peak of the same height can be found on the Atlantic coast of the United States, and from no other point can so fine a view be obtained. "The boundless ocean on the one side, contrasting with high mountains on the other, and along the shore numerous islands appearing like gems set in liquid pearl, form the most prominent features in the scene. White sails dotting the water glide swiftly along What scene could be finer than this, where the two grandest objects in nature—high mountains and a limitless ocean occupy the horizon."

NEWPORT MOUNTAIN is near the water, and also commands a noble view

SOME'S SOUND, an arm of the sea, extends up between the mountain ranges for 7 miles, with a width at its entrance of 2 miles. The scenery has been likened to the Delaware Water Gap, the Hudson River at the highlands and to Lake George, and is a favorite sailing ground.

SOMESVILLE, a small villiage is prettily situated at the head of the sound.

Mount Desert, combines so much that is beautiful that it is difficult to convey to any one an adequate idea of its grandeur.

"An Isle of mountains, hills and dells,
 All rumpled and uneven,
With green recesses, sudden swells
 And odorous valleys driven
So deep and straight, that always there
 The wind is cradled to soft air."
E. B. BROWNING.

Here the tourist will find combined, all the attractions of a country, sea-shore and mountain trip, and the only place on all our Atlantic coast which does combine them.

SOME'S SOUND.

Here the lofty cliffs look down not upon bay or lake, but upon broad ocean. To visit this wondrous island is to " find in one, t l e Isles of Shoals and Wachusett, or Nahant and Mouadnock, or Newport and the Catskills." All that come here come to have a good time, and there is a delicious freedom, an absence of stiffness and severe propriety, w l ich is quite characteristic of the place.

The visitor will be reluctant to leave t l e attractions of this Mountain Island THE RETURN TOUR (leaving Bar Harbor about 10 A. M.) gives a delightful opportunity of witnessing its picturesque scenery by dayligl t, arriving in Portland the evening of the same day.

ATLANTIC HOUSE,

BAR HARBOR,

MOUNT DESERT ISLAND,

MAINE.

This House was opened to the public June 20th, 1874, and is pleasantly located within seven minutes' walk of the Steamboat landing. It contains 44 sleeping-rooms, large and well-ventilated; several of them communicate with others, thus rendering them desirable for families. The Proprietor has taken great pains in furnishing the same with spring beds, mattresses, an abundance of woolen blankets, and everything desirable for the comfort and convenience of his guests.

THE ATLANTIC HOUSE

IS WELL SUPPLIED WITH

Eagle Lake Water on All Floors,

From Eagle Lake, a beautiful mountain lake of the purest and coolest water, three or four miles from the village, from w l ich an unfailing supply of the best of water is obtained, thus insuring perfect drainage. All must be aware that this is a most important matter, as no good drainage can exist without an unfailing water supply. The drains from this hotel run direct to the sea, and are supplied with a *constant stream of running water*.

The Table is Always Abundantly Supplied

With the best in the market at home and abroad, and a cook of long experience, with as - sistants, is engaged, and he flatters himself that in this respect, the ATLANTIC HOUSE cannot be excelled.

Having had long experience, the proprieter is confident that he can give satisfaction to his guests, and will pledge his best efforts to do so.

CARRIAGES ALWAYS IN WAITING to convey passengers to and from the House.

Special Rate to Stork's Tourists of $2.00 per day—one person in a room. $1.63 per day—two persons in a room. Liberal reduction by the week or season.

JOHN H. DOUGLASS, Proprietor.

PORTLAND TO BOSTON,—EASTERN RAILROAD. Leaving Portland on the return trip South, we enter Scarborough. Three miles from here is SCARBOROUGH BEACH. SACO STATION is the next stopping place; here we cross the Saco River and enter the city of BIDDEFORD, a city of over 10,000 inhabitants. SACO POOL is about 9 miles from the station. Steamer Augusta runs twice daily from the pier below the falls, down the river to the Pool There was formerly a popular belief that whosoever entered the Pool on the 26th of June would be cured of all disease. This date will be too late for our tourists Sojourners here often cross Saco bay in small boats to OLD ORCHARD BEACH, which is plainly visible, and to which a line of Stages run to Saco Station.

OLD ORCHARD BEACH is the finest beach in New England and extends from Saco River to Pine Point, a distance of 10 miles, with a breadth at low water of 300 feet. The sand is very hard and smooth, and affords an admirable drive-way with magnificent and unobstructed view of the ocean for the entire distance. The surf is grand and the bathing perfectly safe, owing to the absence of undertow. Old Orchard is noted for its splendid hotels, which are for the most part admirably conducted. Near the hotels is a beautiful forest-park of lofty foliage, the ground covered with moss and graceful ferns, and decorated with pleasant paths, arbors and rustic adornments. It is said to be a favorite resort for poets and literary people.

Passing through Kennebunk, which has several factories and shipyards, we reach Wells village, which is finely situated on a high ridge overlooking the ocean. Leaving Wells village we soon reach Conway Junction, the point from which we diverged from the main road going north to the White Mountains The remainder of the route to Boston is fully given in the description of the Eastern Railroad, on the mountain tour from Boston to Fabyans.

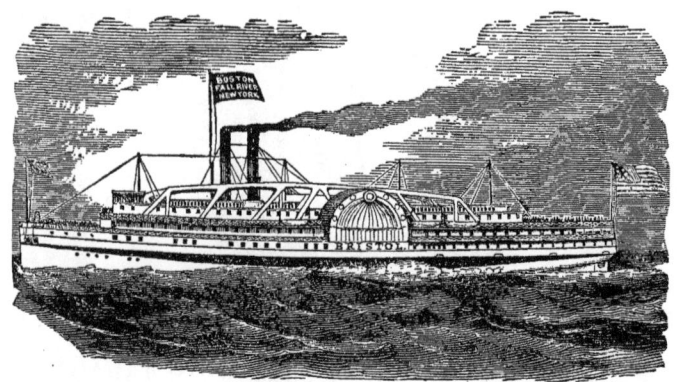

1879 **1879**

EASTERN RAILROAD

THE FAVORITE
SEA-SHORE ROUTE.

Witl its numerous brancles following the NEW ENGLAND COAST, is a string of Ocean Pearls from

BOSTON TO PORTLAND.

No.otler Railroad in the United States, upon an equal lengtl of line, tlreads so many briglt SEA-COAST TOWNS and SUMMER RESORTS. Throughout the heiglt of the season it is literally a summer city, and the ENVIRON OF BOSTON may be said to extend almost to

⇒ MAINE ⇐

The Visitors and Residents of tlis Seaside Region are not drawn from Boston alone, but from all the centres of wealtl in all parts of the land, whose Country-seats and Clateaus along the EASTERN RAILROAD for miles nortl-east of Boston represent the Middle, Soutlern and Western element of the well-to-do and Pleasure-loving.

The Equipment of the Eastern Railroad is Unequalled.
All Modern Improvements in Railroading are Utilized.
Pullman' Celebrated Parlor Cars are run on Day Trains.
All Trains are Controlled by Hall's famous Electric Signals.

IT IS THE ONLY LINE RUNNING

Pullman's Drawing-room Sleeping Cars on Night Trains between BOSTON and BANGOR.

IT IS THE BEST ROUTE TO REACH THE VARIOUS BEACHES:

Manchester by the Sea,   Salisbury, Hampton and Rye Beaches,
The Isles of Shoals,   New Castle,   York.   Old Orchard Beach (via Saco.)
Paland Sprinqs,   Mount Desert,   Rangeley Lakes, and
Mt. Kineo House on Moosehead Lake.

FOR THE

WHITE MOUNTAINS via NORTH CONWAY

AND **THROUGH THE NOTCH** TO THE

CRAWFORD HOUSE, FABYAN'S, PROFILE HOUSE, GLEN HOUSE, BETHLEHEM TWIN MOUNTAIN HOUSE, and last, but not least,

GRAND OLD MOUNT WASHINGTON.

The line of the EASTERN RAILROAD is unsurpassed for Grandeur and Sublimity of Scenery.

TWO DAILY TRAINS from and to BOSTON, witl OBSERVATION CARS ATTACHED, PASS THROUGH THE NOTCH.

Excursion Tickets by this FAVORITE LINE, in connection witl the different Sound Lines and all-rail-routes, can be obtained on application to any of the Agencies of the Pennsylvania Railroad Excursion Tickets at Reduced Rates can also be obtained at the different Offices of the Sound Lines and Railraad Offices generally in New York and at the Eastern Railroad Depot on Causeway Street, Boston.
For furtler information, Special Cars, Reserved Clairs or Sleeping Berths, apply by telegrapl or letter to

JNO. HORNBY,
Master of Transportation.

LUCIUS TUTTLE.
Gen'l Passenger and Ticket Agent, Boston.

STORK'S SUMMER TOURS GO BY THIS ROUTE.

The Baltimore Cash Dry Goods House

IS THE PLACE TO BUY,

FOR THE 6 REASONS FOLLOWING:

1st—We carry a very Superior and Fresh Stock. (Nice Styles of Prints a Specialty.)

2d—A Few Leading Items Not Used as Baits, but sell on Rock-bottom all through Stock.

3d—Nothing put on for Losses by Bad Debts, which is Inseparable from the Credit System.

4th—Sharpest Buyers visiting this Market compose the Great Bulk of Our Trade.

5th—Experience of Patrons is that they can dispose of Our Stuff Readily; and Not be Undersold by Competitors.

6th—We do Not Send Representatives to the Hotels to Bore and Annoy; but shall be Glad to have you call, when in the Market, whether personally acquainted with us or not.

PHILLIPS BROS. & CO.,

WHOLESALE DEALERS IN STAPLE DRY GOODS,

331 and 333 Baltimore St., Four Doors West of Howard, BALTIMORE, MD

CPSIA information can be obtained
at www.ICGtesting.com
Printed in the USA
BVHW070817311218
536770BV00013B/260/P